Poems a La from Wales

Doreen Attwell

A book of poetry by a lady from Wales

Old Bakehouse Publications

First published in August 2013

ISBN 978-1-905967-49-0

Published in the U.K. by
Old Bakehouse Publications
Church Street,
Abertillery, Gwent NP13 1EA
Telephone: 01495 212600 Fax: 01495 216222
Email: theoldbakeprint@btconnect.com
Website: www.oldbakehouseprint.co.uk

Made and printed in the UK
by J.R. Davies (Printers) Ltd.

British Library Cataloguing in Publication Data: a catalogue
record for this book is available from the British Library.

Index

About the author – Doreen Attwell

Doreen Attwell was born in Llanhilleth, South Wales, Great Britain. She is one of ten children born to the Wilcox family who lived in Hyde Place.

Doreen went to work in London after leaving School. But returned to her beloved Wales. She married a local boy and was known as Doreen Goode. She had two children, a son, Philip and a daughter, Marilyn.

Sadly, she was divorced, but a few years later married another local man and had two more children - twins! A son, Mark and a daughter, Mandy. Sadly she was widowed in her early fifties and has remained a widow.

She has three grandchildren, Jason, Matthew and Callum.

Doreen started to write poetry in her forties and the first 45 of her poems are based on true events during her life. She has also written poems about Wales, where she still happily lives in Cwmbran.

Dedication and special thanks

To all of my family:

My two son's Philip Goode and Mark Attwell. My two daughter's Marilyn Lunnon and Mandy Attwell. Marilyn's husband, Stephen Lunnon, Mark's wife, Kerry Attwell and my Grandchildren, Jason Lunnon, Matthew Lunnon and Callum Attwell. Jason's partner Jade Sills and Hayley (her daughter) and Philip's wife Hilary.

And to all of my friends and those I have worked with over the years.

I would like to say a special thank you to my daughter, Marilyn Lunnon for helping me to get my poems published, and my sister's, niece's and nephew's for the photographs.

Finally, Llantarnam Grange staff for their help in finding publishers in Wales. And a big thank you to Janet and staff at the Old Bakehouse Publications, Abertillery for publishing all of these poems.

Thank you all and God bless.

The Six Bells Disaster

To their work that morning
The miners they did go
Going to their place of work
Of disaster they did not know
A great explosion started up
A horrifying blast
Killing men and boy
As they fought to the last
The injured men started to shout
For someone who could get them out
The top of the pit was a mournful sight
Wives and mothers hands clenched tight
Rescue teams went underground
It made them cry at what they found
Why did they die in that great hole ?
Is this the price we pay for coal ?
Was it God's will for them to die ?
If it was, we must know why
At their funeral, thousands did attend
But for these poor lads, it was the end.

The White Cottage

The valley lies smiling before me
The sun over the meadow and sea.
My home is in yonder white cottage
And dear are its memories to me.
Oh where is the valley so verdant
Oh where is the foliage so green.
No place in the wide world
Can match thee.
Oh deep is my pride
And my queen.

The Daffodil

There she stands proudly on a hill
The emblem of Wales, the daffodil
Graceful and tall in golden array
Telling us all spring is on the way
Pretty and slender in colourful tone
Queen of our homeland, you alone
Soon you will leave us
And it will grieve us
Then in the spring
The valleys will sing
You will return and will stand
In our green, pleasant land.

Wales

How green is my valley
The warm scented air
Beautiful green pastures
A sight that's so rare
High are the mountains
Cottages small
This is my homeland
This is my all
Tall are the trees
Their branches spread like wings
Birds sing softly
The joy that nature brings
This is the place I love
The meadows and vales
The place I want to live in forever
My Wales.

Mother

My mother died when I was nine
Too young was I to weep or pine
As I grew older I missed her more
And realised what pain she bore
She had ten children but did not live
To see the pleasures we could give
Why did you die, Mam ?, we need you so
How we miss you, you'll never know
Take good care of her, Lord
Give her the best
Give her thy blessing
And eternal rest.

My Dad

The gates of Heaven are open, Dad
For you to enter through
I watched you suffer all the time
And nothing I could do
You will suffer not in Heaven
So close your eyes to rest
I'll miss you, Dad but realise
It's only for the best
There's another world for you to see
Where there is no pain
God will take you by the hand
Never to suffer again
Look after him, Lord
For though I am sad
Keep him safe in thy keeping
For he is my Dad.

I Believe

Have you lost a loved one ?
If you have, you'll know the feeling that's inside you
    and courage you must show
You realise you're on your own and life must still go on
The grief is so unbearable now that he has gone
Time is a wonderful healer; it helps to win the fight
Each day you will feel better, so try with all your might
You have so much to think of, memories you once shared
These memories live for ever, for those who have always cared
Think of all the good times and of all the pleasure
These will stay within your heart and always you will treasure
Keep your chin up always, be downhearted never
God will not forsake you
He will be your guide forever.

My Friends

If I had to choose between riches and friends, here's what
    my answer would be
I have found all the riches I need in life, just in your company
Gathered round our table and talking of bygone days
Singing songs and old refrains, brings happiness in so many ways
There's a bond between us, no one can bend and contentment
    is ours to treasure
No riches on Earth could buy these things, or could compare
    all our pleasure
Something funny in what we say, we'll start, and then we
    get going
We may get merry, or even tight, the atmosphere is growing
Togetherness means so much to us, a friendship fond and true
No one could ever divide us; we are as one, through and through
I'll raise my glass, to one and all and say these words sincere
God bless, and keep you, dear friends
Through each and every year.

Our Factory

Conway and Stewart, we all know its name
We are the workers, and proud of its fame
We clock in at morning, day just begins
Packing, assembling, filling up bins
Bumping and polishing, and packing too
Getting pens all ready for you
We go to our lunch break; it's time for a rest
Then back to our job to do what is best
Sorting and reaming, no time for dreaming
Banding and capping, boxing and wrapping
All round the world and in far distant lands
We are proud of our work, all done by hands
So this to my workmates I say loud and clear
Keep up the good work, all through each year
You will be praised for a job that's well done
Where we are a family, all classed as one.

My Work friends

Goodbye to you my workmates
It's time for us to part
I'll remember you for ever
You know it breaks my heart
Remember all the good times
That we always shared
Memories live forever
Knowing that you cared
You have been like sisters
Understanding and sincere
The best friends I have ever had
Time is drawing near
Look after yourselves, God bless you
Don't say any goodbyes
Just let me walk out through the doors
With tears in my eyes.

9

Devotion

I *love you when your eyes meet mine*
Across a crowded floor
I love the things you say to me
As we leave to go
I love your sense of humour
And fun we always share
I love to look across the room
And find that you are there
I love the songs we used to sing
So many years gone by
It seems like only yesterday
It makes me wonder why
We had our share of laughter
And of tears too
But the best of all my memories
Are ones I have of you
My dearest dear I say to you
In words so very clear
Good luck, good health, God bless you
I love you more each year.

My Sweetheart

*H**ow can I say in many words how I feel this way ?*
How can I express to you, my love is here to stay
Life is worth the living, knowing that you care
Everything is wonderful, when I know your there
I can carry on in life, if you are there to guide me
Just to know you are there and always beside me
So listen to me when I say you are my life, my all
I'll be there to hear you, anytime you call
Believe me when I say, my dear, till the end is here
You are always in my heart, each day, each month and each year.

10

Companionship

How wonderful to have a family
To share when the day is done
Getting together round a fire
Having lots of fun
All around the piano singing
Songs of bygone days
Spreading happiness about
In so many ways
Friendship is a gift of love
Sincere and so true
Hands reach out to help us
In everything we do
With friends and families around
Life is just worthwhile
Keep your chin up, look ahead
And always wear a smile.

Bliss

I woke up one morning and to my great delight
I opened the window, to a beautiful sight
The birds were all singing a wonderful sound
The sun was shining on all things around
My heart filled with gladness and happy was I
To see all the beauty that money cannot buy
I counted my blessings, it gave me a thrill
To hear church bells ringing from the top of the hill
The sound was enchanting, the choir I could hear
They were singing the Lord's Prayer, it sounded so near
I rarely go to church and seldom do I pray
But hear me Lord, for this I do say
Thank you for the wonderful things and for the joy
and gladness they bring
For surely these wonders are sent from above
The glory of God, and his wonderful love.

The Wisdom of Words

In childhood I learned
The right from wrong
This I remembered
As life went on
Do unto others as they do unto you
Forgive and forget and other things too
Now that I'm older, these words I recall
The wisdom in our heart rules over all
Strengthen my spirit, give me thy word
Believe all these stories that I have heard
Climb every mountain, reach for the sky
Watching the world going swiftly by.

Why ?

Why am I on this Earth, Lord ?
What purpose have I in life ?
The world is full of troubles
Not to mention the strife
Was I sent for a reason ?
If so, tell me this day
Am I to help other people ?
Must I show them the way ?
I am mixed up in this world, Lord
With fear and feeling forlorn
I feel shattered, empty and lonely
Tell me, why I was born ?
Do I give comfort to those who are lost ?
Cheer and love them whatever the cost ?
This I will do, Lord until I am sure
I'm here on this Earth to help the insecure.

Life's Fortune

A gypsy once told me I'd be rich but not with money
I laughed at the time and thought her words were funny
How could she know of the hardships I had and struggles to exist
She couldn't be right, of course, for look what I had missed
My parents were poor; my clothes were shabby
But the gypsy's words were true
We were happy with our lot, although luxuries were few
We would sit round a fire, with a feeling of content
These were the riches of which the gypsy meant
What good is money, if there's no love to share?
Happiness cannot be bought, and is so very rare
So make the most of what you have, whether few or many
You'll be happy with your lot, even without a penny.

I'm Sad

Call it sadness if you may
For this is how I feel
Sadness deep inside my heart
That I cannot heal
I've tried to be like others
And smile at all I see
But a great big wave of misery
Keeps sweeping over me
Tell me to snap out of it
And surely I will cry
For sure enough I try to
I just can't tell you why
The feeling of dismay, the loneliness of life
Is surging right inside me, like a blade of a knife
Who can understand me, who knows how I feel
My heart is heavy, oh dear God, will it ever heal?
Give me strength to carry on and time to find a way
Maybe tomorrow, who knows, will be a better day.

Seasons of Love

I love you in the springtime
As blossom fills the trees
I love you in the summer
Warm days and a gentle breeze
I love you in the autumn
When cold wind turns to rain
I love you in the winter
As the leaves fall in the lane
But most of all, my darling
I love you at Christmas time
I'm yours and you are mine
Greetings I send with lots of cheer
A Merry Christmas and a Happy New Year.

War Time

During the war, many years ago, our men fought hard for their life
We were rationed on food and clothes; it was a matter of struggle
and strife
We had to turn the lights off and to the shelters go
Whenever we heard the sirens, it was to let us know
The enemy planes were about us, ready to destroy our land
We comforted each other, the comradeship was grand
No time was there for hate or greed, each day could be our last
We made the most of every day and so the years went past
The war was over, our men come back, but one thing remains
in our heart
We must live and love and never to hate, for surely that's
how war's start
Never forget, the war may be over and things you can say
when you may
So who do we thank, that our lives were spared ?
Our Lord, God, to whom we must pray.

Retirement

We are sorry you are leaving, your retirement is here
You have always helped us with our work, may I shed a tear
May happiness be yours to stay, forever and a day
All your hopes and dreams come true, as you go on your way
Don't forget to think of us, we wish you all the best
Take things easy for a while, have a real good rest
A new life is ahead of you, it's yours for you to take
We wish you well my dear friend, you deserve a break
Look after your health and be content with all you possess
For you will find peace of mind will bring you happiness
Good luck, my dear, God bless you, spare a thought or two
For those who will really miss you, as we wave goodbye to you.

Our Dad

Dearest Dad, we miss you so
Did you have to die ?
We think of you, and shed a tear
And keep on wondering why
Your life was not a happy one
You lost the will to live
But we, your children, loved you
And hope the Lord, will give
A better life for you in Heaven
Than you had on Earth below
Our thoughts are with you always
And memories will ever grow.

A Thought for Today

Have you ever stopped and stared
And wondered if anyone cared?
Who loves you now for what you are
Whether they are near or far?
There is friendship all around us
If we stop to look, they hear us
Carry on and always smile
Then you'll find that life's worthwhile
I'll walk with God from this day on
His helping hand I'll lean upon
It's just a song, but I believe it's true
And I think that you believe it, too
Helping, caring, sharing and giving
All is part of our everyday living
Never give up and never despair
Always remember someone is there
Go into this world without any sorrow
Live for today and not just for tomorrow.

Forgotten

I'm sitting alone, and wondering why
Maybe there are others as lonely as I
Watching the clock as it ticks on the wall
Time meaning nothing, just nothing at all
People rush by, not a word do they say
To make me feel needed, or brighten my day
Does anyone care, or know how I feel?
Forgotten am I, in a world so unreal
Talk to me stranger, just say a word
Show me you care, let me be heard
A cry for help, don't pass me by
Hold out your hand, lonely am I.

A Boy's Dream

Don't go down the mine, Dad
I have this fearful dread
If you go, of this I am sure
By the end of the day, you'll be dead
His father, with tears in his eyes said these words
My boy, to the pits I must go
For surly you realise this job I must do
To help get coal for the poor
Some old folk have no fire in their grate
So come, lad be brave let us pray
Help us, Lord; keep us safe as we work
Bring us home safely each day
The boy hugged his Dad as he went to his work
Then he went back to his bed
Dear God, don't let me have that dream again
Where I saw my Dad lying dead.

Journey to Forget

Here is the train to take me
Why am I feeling so blue ?
This train is going to take me, far away from you
I should be feeling happy; you're no good to me
Only a heavy burden and so I set you free
You can go to hurt another and maybe break her heart
I'll be miles away from you, it's better we should part
Maybe I'll find another who will be good and true
Then perhaps I'll fall in love, with a love that's new
You go your way, I'll go mine, don't wish me goodbye
I know I must forget you, anyhow I will try
My train is here, I'm on my way, please don't look my way
Let me build a new life
Where happiness will stay.

My Foolish Heart

The dance floor was crowded, the orchestra played
Lights were dim, as everyone swayed
Was it him I saw? It's surely not true
Dancing and swaying with somebody new
Are the lights playing tricks, or my eyes not too clear?
It couldn't be him whispering in her ear
I must find a chair, for surely I'm dazed
It's so unbelievable, I'm truly amazed
He told me he loved me, only last night
Then we had a horrible fight
I lost all control and told him to go
And told him I wanted to see him no more
He cannot see me, so I'll just slip away
Breaking my heart, as I go on my way.

Remembrance

Lord, will you take a message?
To a Dad we loved so sincere
Tell him how much we miss him
His voice we would so love to hear
Is he happy up there in Heaven?
In your kingdom that freed him from pain
If he is, then we are contented
And one day, will meet him again
Let him know we still remember
The songs of his favourite choice
How we would love to hear them
Sung by his own dear voice
Dear face that holds
So sweet a smile for me
Take care of him, Lord
He was our world, you see.

Days of Long Ago

He was merry, gay and light at heart
And fooled me from the very start
His words of love I did believe
With cheating ways he did deceive
How could I go on this way ?
For I knew he'd leave me one day
With hope and courage, years went by
And I look back and wonder why
He was selfish from the start
The day did come and we did part
One day he'll see the wrong of his ways
And maybe feel sorry for the rest of his days
What he did to me, I'll never know why
But one day I'm sure, the heartbreak will die
I will look forward to happier years
No more sadness, no more tears
Help me, Lord, to forgive and trust
Deep in my heart, I know that I must.

A Mother

A mother is a person so gentle and so kind
There's no one quite like her, as you will always find
She's always there to help you, and to her you can turn
If we listen to her advice, there's a lot we can learn
When we have a problem, we ask for her advice
She always tries to help us, isn't that just nice
She comforts us when we are sick, her loving arms reach out
Whatever is wrong, she put's right, of that we have no doubt
I would give up anything, but one thing I would never give up
My dear old Mam, no, not ever.

Homeland

In the cool of the evening
The sun goes down
The valleys are a glorious sight
Much nicer than the town
The silent whisper of a tree
And grass so very green
In the meadows flowers wild
So pretty to be seen
Farmers gathering the corn
Windmills gently turn
The gentle ripple of a brook
And lovely wild fern
This is our countryside in all its glory
Only to see it, tells its own story
How green is my valley
How proud we stand
This is my homeland
This place so grand.

21

Home

Home is where the heart is, whether rich or poor
Home is where there's comfort and a welcome at the door
We take our home for granted as we live from day to day
But home is what we miss most when we are far away
It's nice to get away sometimes and round the country roam
But after a while we start to think, I wish I was at home
Some people live in palaces, some, they live in style
They think that they have everything, it really makes me smile
For when you come to think of it, it isn't where you live
But what goes on inside the home and what we have to give
If you're ever down my way, just call in for a chat
We haven't many luxuries, but there's a welcome on the mat.

My Boy

My little grandson, one year old
He is to me a joy to behold
A happy face full of vim
That's my boy, that's him
He bites my chin, pulls my hair
Pulls himself up from his chair
This lad is strong, a proper boy
But to me a pride and joy
I love him so and hope that he
Always will remember me.

Rest in Peace

It's one year since you left us, Dad
We didn't say goodbye
You were ready to leave us
We never will know why
I expect our Mam was calling you
From the Heaven above
You heard her call and answered
I'm going to join my love
You suffered on this Earth, Dad
But peace comes after pain
Safe in the arms of Jesus
All was not in vain
Now you are together
We will not be sad
For now you are united
Rest in peace; dear Dad.

Not My Day

It was on a Saturday, things went wrong
As soon as I got out of bed, my head did ache
My legs were tired, I wished that I were dead
The washing I did, and cleaned the floor, but I was still in pain
Will I get well? I can't go on, now it's starting again
I go to the bathroom and then I fell, the pain grew worse, I did shout
My family ran to comfort me, it was then I did pass out
To the hospital I went, x-rays were taken
My legs felt worse, I was really shaken
They told me the news, my ankle was broke
With tears in my eyes, I thought I would choke
They put me in plaster and home I did go
But still in my memory
Is that day, long ago.

Childhood

In the eyes of a child
A story is told
The laughter and joy
More precious than gold
They enjoy every second
In wondrous delight
Happiness spreads
When they are in sight
Climbing trees, going wild
This I see in the eyes of a child
We could learn a lot from their ways
For they have such golden days
They are the future with hope in their heart
Living and learning each day apart
Forgive them when they sulk and fight
They will learn the wrong from right
Let them be, weak or wild
We can learn through the eyes of a child.

Our Green and Pleasant Land

Down in our valley, the grass so very green
The mountains and hilltops are a beauty to be seen
People here are very proud, thoughtful and so kind
Where in all the world, would I find such piece of mind ?
The miners are a happy lot as to their work they go
Digging coal for the entire world, their courage we all know
I am proud to be Welsh and sing with all my might
My favourite song I love to hear plays all through the night
Singing gives me comfort as on my way I go
Counting all my blessings, when I'm feeling low
The Lord is my Shepherd, in him I will trust
As I go on life's journey, doing what I must.

Spell Mother

M is for the memories you left me
O is that for others you did care
T is for the time you always gave us
H is for the happiness we did share
E means that everybody loved you
R you were always ready to give

Put these words together, they spell mother
Deep within our heart she'll always live.

Your Mam

To those of you who have a mother
Treat her with gentle care
She is the one you can always trust
And always she is there
Tell her that you love her
When she is depressed
Give to her a helping hand
When she needs a rest
Only one mother you have in life
So give to her the best
As you grow older you realise
You were so nicely blessed
In this life there is no other
Than the love of you, dear mother.

Satisfaction

Who could I turn to, where would I go ?
If I didn't have my home
Life would be empty, that's for sure
Round the country I'd roam
Nowhere to go when the day is done
Only the fields around me
I talk to the trees, but no answers
Just loneliness around me
I gaze at the moon, what do I see ?
Just a light that flickers above
What would I give for a home of my own
And for someone I could love
A month in the open, would open our eyes
To realise, we have all we need
So be content with life as it is
No bitterness, hate, nor greed.

Since You Went Away

Teardrops fall on my pillow
The silent beat of my heart
Since you went and left me
My world is torn apart
How can I have a future
With sorrow and regret
Who can mend a broken heart ?
How can I forget ?
All was going well for us
Then you went away
Leaving a heart that cannot heal
Jut to wither and decay.

Tact

Be careful of the words you speak
For words can be unkind
You must be very tactful
When you speak your mind
Before you say a single word
Be sure it's not bad
For saying spiteful things
Is sure to make one sad
So be sure in what you say
Will not ever offend
Kind words mean so very much
To a dear friend
Let your heart reach out to them
Comfort them today
Remember always, words have meaning
In a special way
The wisdom of words
Is a joy to behold
Sincerity is a blessing untold.

Heartbreak

I saw him last night as he danced round the floor
With tears in my eyes I turned round to go
For I was the girl, he once held so tight
Saying he loved me all through the night
I really believed him, he was so smart
I never thought we would ever part
How could he hurt me this terrible way ?
Surely he realised someone had to pay ?
Love is so blind, for I could not see
Why, oh why, did it have to be me ?
Do I have to go on, with this terrible pain ?
Of knowing he'll never be mine again
I loved him so much and thought he loved me
But he loves another, and wants to be free
I'll give him his freedom, I will not pine
Let him break her heart, as he broke mine
I'll hold back the tears, as I walk through the door
Out of the life of the man I adored.

My Dream of You

In the garden of remembrance
My love for you will grow
A picture I hold in my memory
As time itself will show
Although we are divided
And years will pass away
Deep down within my heart
Your love will always stay
The bond we had between us
Always will remain
Goodnight, God bless, my dearest
Till we meet again.

Our Cat

We had a cat called Sparky
He was black with eyes of green
His fur was long and fluffy
The best you ever seen
When we went out shopping
She would wait out on the street
Until we returned and then
She looked for her special treat
Alas, she grew old and tired
Then one day she died
It broke our hearts to lose her
How I cried and cried
We buried her in our garden
In her favourite spot
Goodbye, dear Sparky
We miss you a lot.

Summer Comes

Summer is coming I can tell by the trees
The beauty of the branches
How green the leaves
The glory of summer
Warm days in the sun
With holidays ahead of us
We are ready for fun
Flowers are blooming in gardens around us
Buttercups and daisies in fields that surround us
The coolness of the evening
A joy to behold
The sky in its splendour
Of blue and of gold
Open your eyes to the world in its glory
For surely these wonders tell their own story.

The Call of Nature

Did you hear a cuckoo
Singing from a tree ?
He is sending you a message
Listen carefully
Start the day with happiness
Spread it all around
Be just like the cuckoo
Make a joyful sound
When the day is dark and grey
Never mind just smile
The sun will surely shine for you
In a little while
All the birds are singing
As they build their nest
Join in their chorus
Come on, do your best
Whistle like a blackbird
Coo like a dove
You have spread the message
In a world of love.

Memory Lane

Down memory lane I wander
To a spot not far away
Where we wandered hand in hand
Happy in every way
We would sit and talk for hours
Our words were that of love
Devoted to each other
The sun shone from above
The love we had was special
I'll go there once again
To recapture magic moments
Down in Memory Lane.

I Wish

If I could have three wishes
And make them all come true
The first would be for you to be
Contented in all you do
My second wish must surely be
That happiness finds your door
And all of those who live within
Bring peace for evermore
For my third wish, let me say
May love come smiling through
For when you have love, you are richly blessed
With treasures and hopes anew.

When a Child is Born

When a baby comes into this world
Its hands are clenched so tight
What will the future hold for him ?
Will it be dark or bright?
He will learn the right from wrong ?
And he will go his way ?
We cannot force upon him
What to do or say
He will find his own way as he goes along
We can only hope that he remains where he belongs
Trusting him will help a lot
And confidence you'll find
Will give him strength of character
Also piece of mind
Be there when he needs you
Show him that you care
And when he grows to be a man
He will be right there.

The Silver Jubilee

Congratulations your Majesty, on this your jubilee year
May you carry on your reign, each and every year
We are proud of your achievement and happy to convey
The way you serve our country, in every single way
God bless you, your highness and let the bells ring out
Your silver jubilee is a success, of that we have no doubt
All over the commonwealth, you are loved by all mankind
Your loyalty and courtesy gives us piece of mind
You show us light when all is dark, our burdens you relieve
And you give hope to everyone and help them to believe
I raise my glass your majesty and hope that you agree
That this is your successful year
Your silver jubilee.

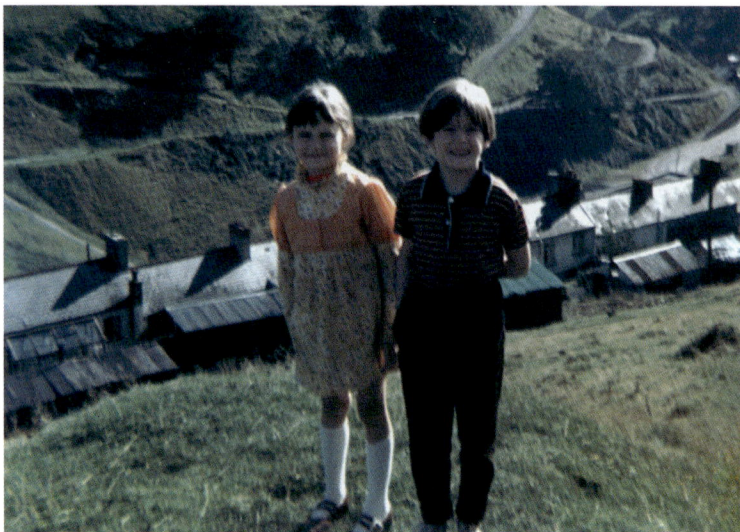

My Twins

*P*eace and quiet is all I need
But I'm all on pins
I haven't had a peaceful day
Since I had the twins
I get them off to school at nine
And to the shops I go
Wash up dishes, making beds
Then I clean the floor
All is quiet, this I love
But it's not to be
For soon the time is four o' clock
The twins are home for tea
TV set is on full blast
What chance have I got
Of getting any quiet
From this noisy lot ?
Maybe one day who knows ?
They'll feel sorry for me
And will be quiet just for once
It would be heavenly.

Stormy Weather

Wind is howling
Rain and sleet
Cold and cheerless
Empty Street
Winter is here with hail and snow
All the trees are bare
Children laughing as they play
They don't have a care
I'm sure it's getting colder
I feel just like ice
Put a log on the fire
Now that's better, nice.

The Gift of Friendship

Please sir, spare a copper for a beggar such as I
A few pence will do sir, there's something I must buy
I have a little boy, just a wee mite
He is just five years old and has lost his sight
I'd like to get a little dog, a present for my lad
It wouldn't cost a lot sir and he would be so glad
What was that you said? £5 you would pay?
God bless you, you're a gentleman
I'll pay you back one day
I'll tell my lad I saw a friend
Who listened to my plea
For a friend in need is a friend indeed
And that's what you are to me.

My Daughter

Although we are divided
We will never be apart.
For I love you so, my dear
From the bottom of my heart.
You are so kind to others
On you they can depend.
I am so very proud of you
A daughter and a friend.
I wish that you lived close to me
I miss you so each day.
I say to God, look after her
In every single way.
Look after yourself, God bless you
You are the world to me.
Never forget I love you
You give me strength, you see.

Our Father

The Lord gave us eyes so we may see
His wonders from above
He gave us lips so we may tell
Of his holiness, his love
Our ears so we may listen
To his songs of praise
Our hands to put together
To thank him for golden days
Then he gave us kindness
So as we may share
Give help, where it's needed
Showing that we care
Most off all, he gave us life
So we may do whatever is right
The road we walk will be steady
Like a candle burning bright.

Optimist

Laugh and the world laughs with you
Weep and you weep alone
Its and old and very true saying
Don't waste time to mourn
All too soon the time will pass
So make it all worth while
It doesn't cost a single penny
To make someone smile
Tell a silly story
Sing a cheerful song
It won't be long they'll all join in
You see, you can't go wrong.

Why Lord ?

Why are people sick, Lord ?
Why are they in pain ?
Where is all your power, Lord ?
To make them well again
We hear of people dying
What did they do wrong ?
Is there nothing you can do ?
To make them all feel strong
All this sadness in the world
Can you put things right ?
Surely you have power, Lord
To help us win the fight
They tell us to believe in God
And he will show the way
He will carry our burdens
If only we will pray
I will go down on my knees
And pray to you tonight
To help the weary and the sick
And show them light.

Kindness

Do a good turn every day
Make someone smile at what you say
Let them know that for them you care
Life is short, so do your share
Sing a song, an old refrain
Join in the chorus, once again
Spread your gladness all around
A new horizon you have found
Keep it up your doing fine
Let happiness be yours and mine.

Dreams

Castles in the air have I
Dreams to be fulfilled
Hope is my ambition
Never to be chilled
Seek the unattainable
Climb up to the moon
And you'll find contentment
All too soon
Seek and you will find
Riches to be found
Never stop looking
There are wonders all around.

A New Year

The season of goodwill has come
Let us not forget
Another year is passed and gone
No sorrow or regret
We will face the future
With trust in all we do
Hold your hands together
It's time to start anew
Do not look behind you
Keep your head held high
Give help where it's needed
Reach up for the sky
Merry Christmas one and all
Let us kneel and pray
Thank you, Lord for giving us
This happy Christmas day.

Life

The way you are in life
Is how you want it so
Do you wish to stand and stare ?
Or to have a go ?
It all depends on you, how you rule your living
You are your own master; it's yours for the giving
We sometimes cannot rule our heart
Nor can we feel glad
But our character shows in what we do
Whether good or bad
Life goes on with our hopes and dreams in store
Who knows what tomorrow brings
What will be the score ?

Silver Lining

Hold your head up high there's a star shining bright
It's shining on you, by day and by night
Watching the way how you live each day
Helping, caring, and showing the way
When you are low, and feeling despair
Look around you, somebody is there
Somebody who needs you, to show you the way
And to help you carry on through each day
Love one another and do what is right
Try to pull through, with all of your might
We all have our troubles, we all have our cares
But somebody, somewhere, has more than their shares
So keep looking up, that star is still shining
Just around the corner, a silver lining.

The Four Seasons

January cold with frost in the air
February snow with trees all bare
March the strong winds that whistle in the night
April showers are in sight
May brings flowers of blue and gold
June starts summer, so we are told
July the holidays are well in sight
August brings the harvest and skies are bright
September leaves fall in the lane
October dark evenings are here again
November days cold and dreary
December the end of the seasons, clearly.

We'll Take a Cup of Kindness Yet

Hark! The sound of sleigh bells ringing
Joyous children carol singing
Trumpets sound ringing in the new
Shout hallelujah! In words so true
Happy New Year we will be proud
Come all ye faithful, sing it loud !
Hold up your head look not around
A new horizon to be found
Let there be light, a new dawn breaking
Dreams and plans, ours for the taking
No time for tears, on this new day
Take your hands, let us pray
Thank you Lord, for a love that shines
For the sake of Auld Lang Syne.

Hope

Give me light so I may see
The glory of God above
Give me strength to carry on
In a world of hope and love
Give me reason to live my life
And never to show despair
Give me fun and laughter
To others, let me care
Give me thy blessing, let me know
You are watching from above
Give me the book so I may read
Of your holiness, your love
Let the light shine from on high
To guide me when I fall
Let me walk through steadfastly
Till the day I hear you call.

A Little Boy's Prayer

A little boy was saying his prayers
Thank you Lord said he
For giving me my Mam and Dad
Without them where would I be ?
I love them so much for what they have done
For you see, I'm their adopted son
With loving care they took me as their own
The happiest family one has ever known
I was found on a doorstep six months old
Suffering with the terrible cold
They took me into their home, I'm glad
And proud to call them Mam and Dad.

Winter

Winter is here I can tell by the trees
Bare are the branches
Bitter cold breeze
Damp, frosty mornings
Dark is the sky
Snowflakes are falling on mountains up high
Clatter of thunder followed by rain
Beating on the window pane
Winter is here but do not despair
The season of spring will soon be in the air.

A Soldier's Last Wish

A soldier lay dying on the battle field
Blood poured from his head
Don't let me die like this, Lord
I have this fearful dread
His comrades tried to soothe him
They knew his death was near
Kind words they said to comfort him
Then he spoke quite clear
Take a message to my Mam
Tell her I was brave
A single tear fell from his eyes
They led him to his grave
Another young life is taken away
Was this the price he had to pay ?
Life goes on, so shall it be
We know not what the end will be.

A Day Out

Children playing in the sand
Lovers walking hand in hand
Harbour lights across the bay
Evening falls, another day
Sun goes down, a gentle breeze
Not a sound among the trees
Kiddies tired, mothers worn
Time to retire, till the dawn
Who knows what tomorrow brings
Many more exciting things
Getting sleepy, eyes shut tight
Just one thing more
Goodnight.

Be Happy

Happiness is a gift to treasure
Smiling always gives us pleasure
Laugh at all you do and say
Taking life the easy way
Time goes quickly when you're glad
Don't be downhearted, or even sad
Spread the atmosphere all around
Let your feet jump from the ground
Shout hooray! This very day
I'm feeling good and so I say
Join me now and sing out loud
I am singing on a cloud
Walk along, with head held high
Count your blessings, reach for the sky !

When the War is Over

Mary and Johnny were sweethearts and planned to wed one day
But Johnny was called to the war and soon would be away
Mary saved hard for the wedding and wrote to her darling each night
She told him she would love him forever and all would turn out right
Johnny fought hard for his country and so the years slipped away
Mary bought a cottage, for he would be home any day
The good news arrived at last, the war was nearly over
Mary got so excited and went to meet Johnny at Dover
They cried when they met, they had so much to say
To make up for the years, when Johnny was away
Wedding bells will chime today
For Mary and Johnny, may your happiness stay.

Fortune

If I had a million pounds this is how I'd use it
I'd give a share to all my friends, be careful not to lose it
I'd go for a cruise on the QE2
See how others live, watch my dreams come true
I'd buy a little cottage, with roses round the door
With all these things around me, who could ask for more ?
Until then I'll be content with all that I possess
There's one thing money cannot buy
That is happiness
I'll count my blessings one by one, and pray to God above
Thank you, Lord, for what I have and giving me your love
As long as I am on this Earth, I'll do whatever is right
It won't be very easy, Lord, but I'll try with all my might

Wedding Day

You have taken your vows
And are now man and wife
A new dawn begins
Into your future life
You will walk together, facing good and bad
Helping each other, and always be glad
The life you have must be full of sharing
Comfort one another, never stop caring
God bless you both
On this special day
May the light from on high
Show you the way.

Spring

Spring is here, blossoms on the trees
Butterflies in the air, and a gentle breeze
A feeling of enchantment, the ripple of a stream
All adds up like the wonder of a dream
Birds are nesting in the trees, now they know its spring
They are happy in their work, as they start to sing
Children playing in the park, they haven't got a care
They all seem to know the feeling, spring is in the air
Let us join them in their fun, let us have a fling
Come on, altogether shout
Here comes spring!

I Remember

There is a green hill far away
I remember it well in a sad kind of way
High mountains, green pastures, clear blue skies
I think of it now, with tears in my eyes
A little grey cottage along the moor
My Mother and Father, they were so poor
They taught me to give, and always to share
Show kindness to others, always to care
These things I remember, now they are gone
But fond are the memories that linger on
I will go there again, I know that I will
To the little grey cottage on the hill
Gone are my loved ones, but still I recall
Things they taught me, when I was small
We shall meet again, in the beautiful land
In the kingdom of Heaven, we will walk hand in hand.

Silver Wedding

The years have gone by
Since you were joined man and wife
The joy and the heartaches
You shared in your life
Together you walked
Through the stairway of love
Two hearts in one
As he watched from above
And so the years passed
You'll look back and say
Is it really 25 years
Since our wedding day?
You have weathered the storm
So I'd just like to say
Happy anniversary
On your silver wedding day.

All God's Children

Monday's child has a heart of gold
Tuesday's child is a joy to behold
Wednesday's child is full of love
Thursday's child has blessings from above
Friday's child does what is best
Saturday's child is richly blessed
And the child that is born on the Sabbath day
Is pure and kind in every way.

Colours

The colour of the sky is blue
With grey at times, and golden hue
Green is the grass, leaves of brown
Stars of silver, like a crown
Rose's red, daisies white
Blossom pink, a glorious sight
Yellow are buttercups, pretty and gay
Crocuses purple, spring on the way
Black are the clouds, on a cold winter's morn
Cream coloured face, on a child that is born
Light is my heart, when I know that it's spring
Bright is the light, the joy that colours bring.

My Valentine

Tell me that you love me
Say those words divine
Whisper to me softly
You're my valentine
Hold me gently in your arms
And tell me that you care
For then I'll know for sure, my love
We are a perfect pair
Let me hear you say once more
I'm yours and you are mine
Take my hand my dearest dear
You're my valentine
You can make me happy
With your lips so sweet as wine
For you know I love you
You're my valentine.

Yesterday

Remember how we used to stroll along a country lane ?
Hand in hand, across the fields, happy once again
We will forget the bad times when things were not so good
And we parted for a while because we thought we should
What went wrong, I'm wondering? Perhaps we were too young ?
For the words we spoke were cruel, of a bitter tongue
Now we are much older and wiser I am sure
No time for bickering we will not endure
Life is what you make it, so live and do your best
Forget the days that were not too good, just let it rest
The future will be good, for we have learned to say
Sorry for the mistakes I made
That was yesterday.

Hold up your Head

Walk along the sunny side
Never mind the rain
Just pretend the sun is shining
You'll feel fine again
Do not walk in shadows
Darkness comes too soon
Get out early in the day
Make believe its June
Be not afraid to smile a while
At everyone you meet
Let them know your walking
On the sunny side of the street
Spread your laughter
Tap your feet
We will follow
To the end of the street.

A Brides Thoughts

The Bride stood at the alter
In a gown of satin and lace
With trembling hands she made her vows
Not a smile upon her face
Her thoughts were of her loved one
Of their days and future in life
Will I be happy, these vows will I keep ?
Am I sure I can be a good wife ?
Her husband turned to her and smiled
He took her hand in his own
The future we will face together
You will never walk alone
They left the church, man and wife
The sun shone down from above
With tears in their eyes, they tenderly kissed
They could face anything with their love.

A Time to Remember

Remember man, as you pass by
The day will come for you to die
Be not afraid, just let it be
There in the great eternity
Peace will come in all its glory
Like a legend of a story
As we are born
So we must die
And never to know
The reason why.

Happy New Year

Memories old, memories new
Sentimental days, fond and true
A baby born, a marriage vow
We recall them here and now
Let the New Year bring us peace
Friendship and kindness never to cease
Do not forget what has passed and gone
All too soon, time passes on
Someone we loved maybe, gone forever
Yet somehow we forget them never
Ring out the old, ring in the new
Blessings we send to those we knew
Reach out your hands for Auld Lang Syne
A cup of kindness, filled with wine
Another year, passed and gone
But memories will linger on
Take your glass, and say with cheer
Welcome to another year !

Eventide

The moon, as it rises over the hill
Gives us light on a night that is still
Not a murmur we hear, no breeze in the air
No flickering shadows, just emptiness there
Time stands still on a night such as this
Giving us memories of sheer bliss
A time to recapture and recall
The words of our Lord, who rules over all
Surely goodness shall follow me
All of my life, so shall it be.

Life Hereafter

Do not be afraid to die
When God calls you home
Take his hand
And in his garden you will roam
You will see the beauty
In the glory of his love
Peace will be forever
In his heavenly home above
So, when the time comes
Be not afraid to go
The Lord will be waiting
And he opens up the door
For you to enter into
A far and better land
Peace is yours forever
As he takes you by the hand
Be not afraid, but happy
You will feel no pain
In the kingdom of our Lord, you will remain.

21 Today

You are 21 and hopes held high
Your dreams come true if only you try
A life full of laughter, joy to be found
Spreading happiness all around
This is your day, the key of the door
Open your heart where love is in store
God bless you now, and let each day
Be filled with gladness along the way.

Diamond Wedding

Two people in love after sixty years
This is a joy to behold
Lots of laughter and many a tear
You will never grow old
For when you are loved
You have something to treasure
Age has no meaning
But a life filled with pleasure
Caring and sharing
In all kinds of weather
Good times and bad times
Always together
Wonderful memories are yours on this day
For you to share in a special way
Congratulations and all the best
A perfect couple richly blessed.

Love

Love is the reason for giving and sharing
Helping others and never stop caring
Listen to their troubles and you will find
The love you give to others gives you piece of mind
Life is too short for greed or hate
Give help where it's needed before it's too late
Reach out your hands in loving care
Let someone know their burdens you will share
Give unto others and they will give you
A friendship as pure as early morning dew.

Our Diana

We loved you so, Diana
Your memory will linger on
You helped the weary and the sick
To us you will never be gone
Your loving smile and tender touch
Won the heart of us all
As we, the nation, mourn you
You made your curtain call
A true Princess is what you were
Loyal in every way
Happiness was nearly yours
Until that fateful day
We cry for you in the valleys and dales
You truly were the Princess of Wales.

Our Yesterdays

Those were the days when we were young
Fun to be had, songs to be sung
Living and loving each day apart
Goodness that came from a warm, loving heart
We remember those times when older we grew
No one can take those memories we knew
We still have good times, and look at each day
To a warm, sunny future
To enlighten our way.

Little Boy's Prayers

A little boy was saying his prayers
And this is what he said
Thank you Lord for giving me
The warmth of my sweet bed
Thank you Lord for giving me
Your wisdom from above
Thank you Lord for giving
Your loyalty and love
Thank you Lord in Heaven
For all eternity
Thank you for my precious eyes
For all the world to see
And when the day is over
I thank you Lord for Rest.

Birthday Love

To a very special person on a very special day
I have a special message I'd like to convey
Have a lovely birthday with family all around
Be content with all you have and riches you have found
The Lord is watching from above to guide you on your way
Let happiness be yours, my dear in a special kind of way.